DM

Erin

Leung

THE SECRET WORLD OF

Wolves,
Wild Dogs,
and Foxes

THE SECRET WORLD OF

Wolves,
Wild Dogs, and Foxes

Theresa Greenaway

RAINTREE
STECK-VAUGHN
PUBLISHERS

A Harcourt Company

Austin   New York
www.raintreesteckvaughn.com

Copyright © 2001 Steck-Vaughn Company

Published by Raintree Steck-Vaughn Publishers, an imprint of Steck-Vaughn Company

Acknowledgments
Project Editors: Sean Dolan and Kathryn Walker
Consultant: David Larwa
Illustrated by Robert Morton
Designed by Ian Winton

Planned and produced by Discovery Books

Library of Congress Cataloging-in-Publication Data

Greenaway, Theresa, 1947-
Wolves, wild dogs, and foxes / Theresa Greenaway..
p. cm. -- (The secret world of--)
Includes bibliographical references (p.).
ISBN 0-7398-3507-6
1. Wolves--Juvenile literature. 2. Wild dogs--Juvenile literature. 3. Foxes--Juvenile
literature. [1. Wolves. 2. Wild dogs. 3. Foxes. 4. Canidae.] I. Title.

QL737.C22 G727 2001

599.77--dc21   00-062829

Printed and bound in the United States
1 2 3 4 5 6 7 8 9 LB 05 04 03 02 01

Contents

CHAPTER 1
Introducing the Dog Family

The fennec, a long-eared fox that lives in Africa and the Middle East, is the smallest member of the dog family, with a head and body length of only about 15 inches (38 cm), and an 8-inch (20 cm) tail. It weighs just 3 pounds (1.4 kg).

A large gray wolf can measure over 6 feet (about 2 m) from its nose to the tip of its tail. It can weigh 176 pounds (80 kg).

The long-legged maned wolf is the tallest member of the dog family, standing about 35 inches (90 cm) at the shoulder.

The Arctic fox can survive in temperatures as low as -76 degrees Fahrenheit (-60 degrees Celsius).

Before it was exterminated in many parts of its range, the gray wolf was the most widespread species of the dog family.

Wolves, wild dogs, and foxes make up what is usually called the dog family. Together with other families of mammals, such as the cats, bears, and seals, the dog family belongs to the carnivores, or flesh-eaters. Wolves, wild dogs, and foxes are scavengers as well as predators, and they are not all exclusively meat eaters. Many also eat fruit and insects.

There are about 34 living species of wolves, wild dogs, and foxes. Our pet dogs, no matter what their size, shape, or pedigree, are all descendants of one of these wild species—the gray wolf. Except for wolves, which can be quite large, most dog species are small- to medium-sized mammals with long legs and a thick coat of fur. The head shape of all wild members of the dog family is similar. They each have a long muzzle, forward-looking eyes, and large furry ears. Most wolves, wild dogs, and foxes have tails that are long and bushy. The raccoon dog and the bush dog are exceptions. These have somewhat short tails.

▶ A typical wild dog, fox, or wolf, like the gray wolf seen here, has sturdy legs, dense fur, and a long muzzle for holding onto prey.

Nose
A healthy member of the dog family has a wet nose to enable it to detect airborne smells.

Eyes
A wolf's eyes are positioned so that it can judge distances accurately.

Ears
These large, furry ears can twist around to pick up sounds from all directions.

Tail
A long, bushy tail helps a wolf to keep its balance when chasing prey.

Fur
A thick coat of fur keeps the wolf warm, but in summer some of this fur is shed, or molted, so it does not overheat.

Claws
Strong claws dig into the ground when the wolf runs, helping it to keep a steady footing.

The color of the dog's fur varies from white to gray, tawny brown, or sandy brown. The gray wolf can vary from almost white to a much darker, brownish gray. Arctic foxes may be pure white in winter but turn a brown color in summer. Wolves, wild dogs, and foxes live all around the world, from the Arctic tundra in the north to the hot

▲ Unlike most other members of the dog family, the African wild dog is dappled all over with patches of black, white, and sandy yellow.

◀ The fur of the fennec is the same color as the sandy desert in which it lives.

deserts of Africa, North America, and Asia. Only Australia and Antarctica have no native dogs, wolves, or foxes. The dingo was introduced to Australia by people 4,000-8,000 years ago. More recently, red foxes have been introduced there from Europe.

The red fox is now the most widespread member of the dog family, living in Europe, North America, much of Asia, and parts of Africa, as well as its new Australian home.

▼ Although most red wolves have reddish brown fur, some may be black.

▲ The Australian dingo may tolerate human company, but it is not easily domesticated.

8

WHO'S WHO?

There are only two kinds of true wolves, the gray wolf (also called the timber wolf in the United States) and the red wolf. Genetically, wolves are virtually identical to domestic dogs. Their other closest relatives are jackals, coyotes, and dingoes. There are about 14 different species of foxes, most of which live in the northern hemisphere. In addition to well-known species of wild dogs such as jackals and coyotes, there are less familiar kinds such as the dhole, which lives throughout East Asia; the raccoon dog of eastern Europe and Asia; the bush dog of South America; and the African wild dog.

Gray wolves in one part of the world differ in size and color from those in another. The gray wolves on Ellesmere Island in the Canadian Arctic, like this one, are white.

OUT AND ABOUT

Wolves, wild dogs, and foxes spend most of their time on the ground. They have amazing stamina, and most can travel for long distances at a trot. During the final stages of a hunt, or while escaping from danger, wolves, wild dogs, and foxes run very fast, using their long tails to help them keep their balance when turning. Like most mammals, wolves, wild dogs, and foxes are usually good swimmers.

Wolves, wild dogs, and foxes walk and run on their toes. They have leathery pads and sturdy, blunt claws. These strong claws are not retractable (able to be pulled back). They dig into the ground as the animal trots and runs, which helps the animal to keep its footing. Members of the dog family are efficient diggers. Using their front legs and claws, they dig into hard, dry soil to find food or make a den.

THE RIGHT TEMPERATURE

Even in cold weather, wild dogs, wolves, and foxes get hot after a chase. All members of the dog family open their mouths and pant to give off excess body heat. As moisture evaporates from the tongue, it cools the animal down. Many shed or molt their fur in spring, regrowing it in late summer. Species that live in the desert or on the savannah (African grasslands), such as the fennec

Foxes are more agile than other wild dogs. Some, such as the red fox seen here, even climb trees.

and bat-eared fox, have very large ears. Besides aiding hearing, large ears help to reduce body temperature because they provide a large surface area for heat loss.

Dog species that live in places with bitterly cold winters have the opposite problem. They have to keep warm, even when it is snowing. Gray wolves, raccoon dogs, and especially Arctic foxes have very

The gray wolf can run steadily for many miles without getting tired.

thick winter coats with dense underfur to keep them warm. The Arctic fox also has tufts of fur between its toes and small, very furry ears. It fluffs out its fur to increase the insulating layer of warm air it can hold. When sleeping, the Arctic fox curls up in a ball and wraps its bushy tail around its face.

CHAPTER 2
Keen Senses

Wolves, wild dogs, and foxes are constantly on the alert for danger. They are also always on the lookout for opportunities to catch or find something to eat. Most wild dogs and foxes are small enough to be at risk themselves from larger predators, including wolves. To keep themselves safe and well-fed, wolves, wild dogs, and foxes rely on their keen senses of sight, hearing, and smell.

The African wild dog hunts in daylight or by the light of the full moon. It has keen eyesight and ears that pick up the noises made by possible prey.

Dogs have as many as 220 million scent-sensitive cells in their noses. Humans have around 5 million.

A coyote can hear sounds of much higher pitch than humans—as high as 80 kHz. Humans can hear sounds of up to only 20 kHz.

Long, stiff whiskers on the dog's snout are sensitive to touch and also detect movements in the air. This means that even in complete darkness, a dog knows when something gets too close.

During daytime, a fox or wild dog can use its eyes to hunt and detect danger, but many species are at least partly nocturnal. In darkness, highly sensitive hearing and an acute sense of smell are essential. Coyotes and red foxes are naturally active during the day, but have become more active by night to avoid hazardous encounters with people. Fennecs are truly nocturnal, hiding by day in their dens to avoid the hot desert sunshine. Night can be a good time to hunt, since this is when large beetles, frogs, toads, and rodents are most active.

The eyes of animals that have a *tapetum lucidum* shine brightly when a flashlight or car headlights are aimed at them at night.

EYESIGHT

The eyes of wolves, dogs, or foxes are positioned to give a wide field of view, with good binocular vision, so that they can judge distances accurately. Their eyes are suited to day or night activity. To help them see at night, wolves, dogs, and foxes have a layer at the back of their eyes, the *tapetum lucidum*, that reflects back light that has passed through the retina. This helps them see in the dark, and it is responsible for the "eyeshine" that occurs when light shines on a dog's eyes at night. Wolves, dogs, and foxes can see some colors, but their color vision is not as good as that of human beings.

HEARING

All members of the dog family have large outer ears. The ears can twist around to pick up sounds from all directions. A good sense of hearing is most important after dark. Wolves, dogs, and foxes can detect sounds over a far wider range than humans, particularly at higher frequencies.

A bat-eared fox eats a lot of insects and other small animals. Its hearing is so good that it can hear the rustlings made by prey buried in the ground, so it knows just where to dig.

SENSE OF SMELL

Wolves, dogs, and foxes rely very heavily on their sense of smell. They can detect and identify the slightest trace of a scent. They can track prey by following slight traces of the scent left by its paws. A healthy dog's nose is always wet so that airborne smells can be detected more effectively. This moisture comes partly from secretions inside the nostrils, but foxes, wolves, and dogs also lick their noses to keep them moist.

SCENT MARKING

Wolves, wild dogs, and foxes also use smell to recognize each other. Each animal has its own individual smell, which is produced by glands near the tail. Some of these glands make the smelly secretions that give a characteristic smell to dog or fox droppings. Wolves, dogs, and foxes often deposit their droppings and urinate in conspicuous places, using them as territorial markers. Marking their territory like this is a way of letting others know where they live. Urine also contains chemicals that convey information about the sex of an individual, and whether it is ready to breed.

I DIDN'T KNOW THAT

Dog Talk

All wolves, wild dogs, and foxes use voice and body language to communicate with each other. Only wolves, jackals, and coyotes throw their heads back and howl, but these and the rest of the dog family have a range of barks, yelps, whines, and growls, all with different meanings. Wolves, dogs, and foxes indicate their mood by body posture and facial expression. A submissive animal that does not want to fight adopts a low posture, with its ears down and its tail between its legs. It will roll onto its back as a final gesture. Dominance is shown by standing tall, with the fur on the back of the neck and shoulders raised, tail held flat, ears pricked, and teeth bared. When two animals recognize each other, they wag their tails and jump about playfully.

Dominance

Submission

CHAPTER 3
The Pack

Wolves routinely cover more than 10 miles (16 km) of territory a day.

African wild dogs hunt over an area as large as 380 square miles (1,000 sq km).

Before disease and hunting by humans greatly reduced the African wild dog population, a pack might contain as many as 100 animals.

Gray and red wolves, African wild dogs, and dholes are social animals that live in groups called packs. Members of the pack work together to hunt, protect themselves, and rear the young. The area that a pack occupies is called its territory. Territories have to be large enough to contain enough food to support the pack. If an area is rich in prey animals, then a territory may be quite small. In places such as the Arctic tundra, prey animals are few and far between. A wolf territory is fiercely guarded. Its boundaries are scent-marked and are frequently patrolled by members of the pack. Any intruder will be attacked if it does not retreat immediately.

Wolves do not hibernate in cold winter weather. They need to keep on hunting or they will starve to death.

Coyotes, jackals, and dingoes may also hunt together in small packs or family groups, but these groupings are temporary and break up when the young animals move away from their parents to start life on their own. During the time the family is living and working together as a pack, the young learn the hunting skills necessary to survive and start their own families.

Why do such fierce carnivores live in packs? Living in a pack has great advantages, particularly for hunting, food-gathering, finding shelter, safety, and raising the young. Living together even helps

A family of dingoes hunt together in the Australian bush to bring down kangaroos and wallabies.

animals stay warm in cold weather. Smell, body language, and vocal communication all help to unite the members of a pack, and all individuals have a part to play in the life of the pack community. Even our domestic dogs still have the instinct to live in packs. Especially in big cities, dogs that are lost or have been abandoned get together to form a pack that scavenges for food together. These packs are made up of dogs of all shapes and sizes.

STRUCTURE OF A WOLF PACK

A wolf pack may be small, with only a few animals, or quite large, with 12 or more adult wolves. There is a complicated social structure. The strongest male is dominant and is known as the alpha male. Together with his mate, the alpha female, they are the dominant pair. Only this pair usually breed, although in times of plenty, other pairs may separate from the main pack and breed, forming family groups. All pack members help to look after and feed the pups.

The alpha-male wolf is always ready to defend his position in the pack. Other males are quick to adopt a submissive posture during social contact so that they do not get injured.

The position of the dominant pair is always uncertain. Although they enjoy high status, they are constantly challenged by younger animals. The dominant male holds his position only while he is in peak condition. As soon as he is past his prime, he is replaced by a younger, fitter male. Similarly, younger females are always ready to replace the alpha female.

HOWLING

Most kinds of domestic dogs bark and only rarely howl, but wolves howl, and do not bark. A large territory is important to the survival of a wolf pack, but fighting off an invading pack would be damaging. So to let each other know where they are, packs use howling as a means of communication to avoid territorial disputes. Howling also helps animals that have become separated from the pack to find each other again.

Wolves howl after a successful kill. One animal starts howling, then the rest of the pack joins in. The sound travels for miles across grasslands or through forests.

AFRICAN WILD DOG PACKS

Packs of African wild dogs usually number between 10 and 30 animals, although they used to be much larger before the overall population of African wild dogs was so greatly reduced. The social structure of these packs is very much like those of other wild dogs, especially wolves. Only the dominant couple, the alpha male and alpha female, breed. This couple usually pairs for life. The rest of the pack, both males and females, serve as helpers, especially in raising the offspring of the alpha couple. The helpers will continue to care for the young dogs even if one or both of the parents is killed, dies, or becomes separated from the pack.

HUNTING IN A PACK

By working together, dogs in a pack are able to kill much larger animals than they can on their own. Packs of wolves, African wild dogs, and dholes identify young or weakened deer, antelope, or other prey and stalk them. They separate their intended victim from the rest of its herd. If it is a newborn animal, it may be overcome quickly. Otherwise, they give chase. Most herbivores can out-run their predators if they are in peak condition, but packs of wolves and wild dogs have great stamina and pursue a victim for some miles. Eventually, an old, sick, or injured animal succumbs.

African wild dogs hunt by sight in a closely organized pack to bring down animals such as Thompson's gazelles or impalas. During a chase, the pack trots about 10 minutes, then speeds after its prey at up to 30 miles (48 km) per hour. The dogs take turns to lead, and the pack cuts corners to gain on prey. Hunting in this organized way has a high success rate.

A pack of African wild dogs will even pursue its victim into shallow water in order to make a successful kill.

The Whistling Dog

A pack of dholes consists of 5 to 12 animals. Dholes hunt by day and make a variety of calls at different stages of the chase. When the pack is scattered, they make a whistling sound to keep in contact. As they come together to pursue one animal, dholes run in silence if they can see each other, but the leaders yap if the pack is running through undergrowth. As they close in on their quarry, the yapping increases. Dhole packs are fearless, even attacking and killing bears and tigers, although its usual prey is wild deer.

Large prey is brought down either by bites to its flanks and legs, or by one of the pack hanging onto its muzzle. Wolves and wild dogs are not speedy killers, and unlike members of the cat family, do not kill their victim by crushing the throat. The pack generally kills a big animal by biting out its stomach.

CHAPTER 4
Living in Pairs

Foxes and most wild dogs live a more solitary life than wolves and do not form large packs. Some, such as maned wolves, coyotes, and foxes spend a large part of every year alone, although males and females often have territories that overlap. They pair up just to breed and rear their young, with the males helping to provide food for their pups.

Arctic foxes, raccoon dogs, bush dogs, and jackals are among those that often live as a pair all year round. Many pair for life, and maintain a close bond, strengthened by constant contact and activities such as mutual grooming. Very often, as in the case of golden

Mutual grooming maintains the bond between a male and female golden jackal. It also helps them to keep their fur in good condition.

A male jackal may travel 25 miles (40 km) or more in just one night to find food for his pups.

Unlike other wild dogs, the maned wolf is not good at digging. It makes its dens in thick scrub, under fallen trees, or in small caves.

The Bengal fox usually digs its dens into open ground, but in areas likely to flood, it chooses a hill or mound.

In India, the golden jackal lives at altitudes up to 12,000 feet (3,650 m) in the Himalayas.

In spite of a very thick coat of fur, the raccoon dog sleeps in a den during the coldest winter weather.

jackals, a pair and their pups will hunt together as a family group until the pups leave home.

The amount of territory needed by these smaller foxes and wild dogs is much less than that needed by wolves. A pair of black-backed jackals, for instance, has a territory of up to 1 square mile (2.5 sq. km), but the size of the territory depends on the availability of food. Plenty of prey means that a smaller territory will support a pair and their pups in the breeding season.

THE RACCOON-LIKE DOG

Raccoon dogs are one of the least dog-like members of the dog family. They have short legs, fairly small ears, and raccoon-like face markings. They live in thick woodlands, where they rest by day in a den dug into the ground. It is thought that raccoon dogs stay in pairs throughout the year. As the weather cools in autumn, they fatten up on seeds and berries, then hide away in their den to pass the cold winter months. Although they sleep much of the time, they come out to feed whenever the weather is warm enough.

Dogs of the Jungle

The now very rare bush dog lives in the evergreen forests of southeast Brazil and Paraguay. A male and female form a strong bond and bring up their pups together. Their long, low-slung body and short legs make them ideally suited for pursuing rodents such as pacas through the undergrowth and even into the paca's burrow. To mark their territory, bush dogs urinate standing on their front legs up against a tree.

A SOLITARY LIFE

Outside the breeding season, many foxes live by themselves. This helps to ensure that there is enough food to go around. Because the female has to stay close to her helpless pups for the first few weeks of their life, she needs the help of a mate to bring food. The red fox does not pair for life. Female foxes, called vixens, fight each other fiercely to win possession of a particularly good territory. Male foxes, called dogs, fight each other to win access to both the territory and the vixen. These fights ensure that only the fittest foxes breed successfully.

HUNTING

Jackals and coyotes, like wolves and dholes, can maintain a steady trot for mile after mile without tiring. If the prey they hunt is scarce, they need to cover a lot of ground in order to find enough food to eat. Black-backed jackals work as a pair when trying to make a catch of a newborn antelope calf. One jackal distracts the female antelope, while the other snatches her calf.

Jackals and coyotes hunt prey in family groups, but the smaller foxes pursue smaller prey that do not need the strength of a pack to overcome. These smaller animals catch rodents and insects by listening intently and watching for movement, then pouncing, rather like a cat.

This red fox can hear a mouse tunneling under the snow. By pouncing, it hopes to trap the mouse under its front paws and then kill it with its teeth.

CHAPTER 5
Food and Feeding

The main prey of gray wolves living in the Arctic is caribou, or reindeer.

Red foxes living on the slopes of the Himalayas eat acorns when they fall from the trees in late summer.

An adult wolf needs to eat an average of about 9 pounds (4 kg) of food every day.

The crab-eating fox from South America is not very well named. Crabs are just one item on its menu—together with frogs, snails, birds, lizards, insects, fruit, and fungi!

Members of the dog family drink by lapping up water with their long tongues.

Just like domestic dogs, many wolves, wild dogs, and foxes will eat almost anything that comes their way. Those that hunt in packs feed on larger animals such as deer, antelope, and wild pigs when they can catch them, but young rabbits, rodents, and ground-nesting birds and their eggs are often easier to catch or find. Many members of the dog family will also eat carrion— animals that have died naturally or that are the remains of another predator's kill. As more and more roads are built, animals that have been run over by cars have become an important food source.

Wild dogs and their relatives are quick to take advantage of a new source of food. Their diet depends

Foxes take advantage of any good source of food. This fox is eating mussels that are exposed when the tide goes out.

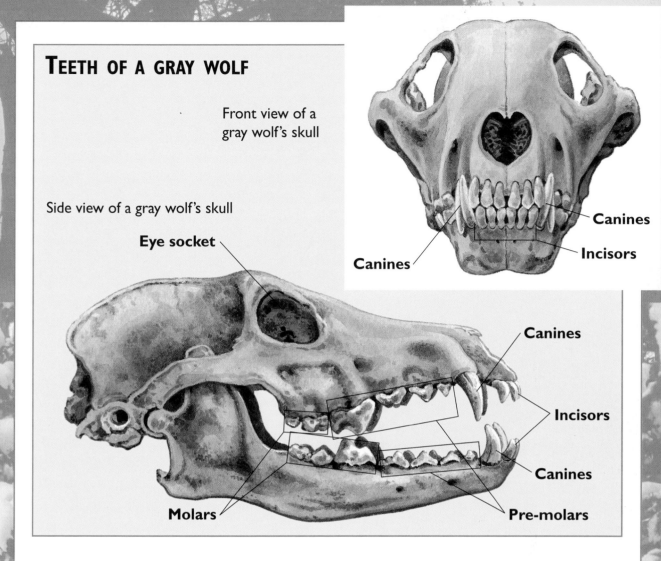

TEETH OF A GRAY WOLF

Front view of a gray wolf's skull

Canines

Canines

Incisors

Side view of a gray wolf's skull

Eye socket

Canines

Incisors

Canines

Molars

Pre-molars

on the time of year. When fruit is in season, the raccoon dog, the maned wolf, and many foxes feast on it. Some foxes even eat leaves as well as fruit. Those that live near water or beside the sea, eat plenty of fish, frogs, or dead animals washed up by the tide.

TEETH

Most members of the dog family have 42 teeth. At the front are chisel-shaped incisors which are used to nibble and groom fur. Four large pointed canine teeth are for holding onto prey, and behind these in the cheek are molars and pre-molars that can shear flesh and bones. A wolf, fox, or wild dog can crunch food to a certain extent, but it usually bolts its food down in chunks, a habit still seen in the domestic dog! They may hold down food with their forepaws so pieces can be bitten off more easily.

CARRION

Most members of the wolf family are not fussy eaters and will eat carrion, animals that are already dead, as well as freshly-killed meat. Jackals in particular steal a lot of their food from other animals, such as cheetahs, harassing them until they abandon their kill. Uneaten dead animals soon start to smell, especially in hot weather. This does not deter animals such as the red fox, which will often dig up dead pets that their unhappy owners have not buried deeply enough.

A red fox will overturn trash cans or tear open garbage bags in order to find morsels of food thrown away by humans.

INSECT-EATERS

Insects are highly nutritious, and they are often abundant and easy to catch, but they are encased in a hard, indigestible outer layer. Bat-eared foxes feed mostly on insects, especially termites, together with fruit and juicy roots. They have more molars than the rest of the dog family, so they can grind up their tough prey. Young pups of all species that are learning to hunt eat lots of beetles, worms, and insects because they are easier to catch.

SCAVENGING

Part of the reason for the successful spread of species such as the red fox is that they will take advantage of any new food source that comes their way, including garbage thrown out by humans. They will raid garbage cans and eat almost everything from cooked meat to curries, fruit tarts, and baked potatoes. The golden jackal also forages for food on garbage heaps.

A Good Store of Food

Even wild dogs and foxes have their fill eventually, so in times of plenty, surplus food is buried. Foxes, jackals, and coyotes all make such food caches. Red foxes dig holes using their forepaws, put the food in the hole, and push the earth back with their noses. They can be very careful about hiding their food—one red fox that buried a dead squirrel dug a hole underneath a plant pot and carefully replaced it when it was done!

I DIDN'T KNOW THAT

CHAPTER 6
Reproduction

Wolves, wild dogs, and foxes usually breed only once a year. Males and females that do not pair for life first need to make contact with each other. The female indicates that she is ready to mate by changes in her behavior and in her scent. Like other mammals, the young develop inside the mother's body until they are ready to be born.

When a pet dog has a litter of puppies, they usually all survive. The mother does not have to search for food. Her owners give her and her pups all the food that they need. In the wild, life is very different. Food is seldom abundant, and there is much competition for it. It requires the

Red foxes mate in winter. For about three weeks, the male and female stay close together. The male fox does not want to let another male near his mate.

The maned wolf produces litters of only 1 to 3 pups.

A gray wolf may produce up to 14 pups in one litter, but 6 or 7 is more usual.

An African hunting dog has as many as 16 pups in one litter, but it is unlikely that all will survive.

In captivity, red foxes live for as long as 13 years, and kit foxes have lived for 20 years.

Foxes live 10 years on average in the wild. Gray wolves live from 8 to 16 years.

A female wolf, fox, or wild dog will not mate unless she is ready. This female wolf is giving the muzzle of the alpha male a nip that means "Go away!"

hunting and foraging skills of a whole pack of wolves or African wild dogs to support just one litter of pups. Males, whether one of a pair or a pack, help to care for the young. Some will regurgitate food for the pups. In other species, such as the red fox, the male brings food close to the female's den and calls to her. If food is scarce, or the male dies, the female, which is known as the vixen, is unable to feed all her pups, and some will die.

FINDING A MATE

Solitary foxes and wild dogs are normally silent, but as the breeding season approaches, males and females need to let each other know where they are. Male foxes bark as they cross a female's territory and leave scent markers for her. Females also leave scent messages. A red fox vixen makes a raucous scream to announce her readiness to mate to the male fox.

BIRTH

Female wolves, foxes, and wild dogs give birth hidden safely in a sheltered den. Good dens are often used for many years, but a female may dig a new one beneath a tree stump, or even beneath an abandoned building. Some use burrows dug and then abandoned by other animals. A deep, low cave among rocks may also be suitable. If the mother feels threatened, she will move her pups to a new den.

As soon as each pup is born, the mother licks the pup to clean it and help it start breathing. Then the mother gives the pups their

A female gray wolf guards her pups as they start to explore the world outside their den. Young animals are very vulnerable to larger predators, including birds of prey.

first meal—her milk. All pups are blind and helpless at birth. They can only crawl slowly and are unable to survive on their own. During this time, the mother stays with them almost constantly.

GROWING UP

After two weeks, the pups' eyes open and they gradually become more active. The mother starts to regurgitate partly digested food for her pups at about one month. When they can move about, the pups emerge from their den and play together outside. Red fox pups start to play outside their den when they are about four weeks old.

HELPERS

In a pack, non-breeding adults help to feed the pups and to protect them from predators. Young pups are very vulnerable from the time that they first emerge from their den until they are full-grown. Larger predators will soon grab an unlucky pup. Helpers use their voice to warn pups of danger, such as an approaching predator, or the approach of an automobile.

Playing

Playing is an important part of the young pups' development. It helps them develop the fast reflexes and other skills necessary to hunt and kill for themselves. They strengthen their jaws by chewing on bones or pieces of fur. As soon as they can keep up, the pups join their parents or the rest of the pack when they go out hunting.

I DIDN'T KNOW THAT

33

CHAPTER 7
Threats and Enemies

The gray wolf has long been feared and hated by many human beings. People who live near wolves, particularly ranchers and farmers, often feel that wolves are a threat to themselves, their children, and their livestock. It is true that wolves and some kinds of foxes and wild dogs do sometimes prey on livestock, but there are very few documented cases of wolves attacking humans. Even so, such

Hunters in Poland carry a wolf carcass from the forest. In European folklore, the wolf is often a symbol of evil, "the big, bad wolf" of fairy tales and legends.

Worldwide, as many as 1.5 million red foxes are caught every year for their pelts.

Half a million gray foxes are caught every year for their fur in North and Central America.

Arctic foxes are still reared on fur farms in countries such as Finland.

Wolves, wild dogs, and foxes defend themselves by biting if they are cornered.

Rüppell's fox lifts its tail and sprays enemies with a vile-smelling liquid from a gland at its rear.

Such poisons as strychnine and Compound 1080, which were once used to kill coyotes, also killed swift foxes, eliminating them in parts of their range.

The white winter pelt of the Arctic fox is still used to make fashion garments. Arctic fox farms provide millions of pelts every year, reducing numbers caught in the wild.

fears have resulted in gray wolves being eliminated from many parts of their former range and brought to the brink of extinction in other areas. Gray wolves disappeared from parts of Europe in the 18th century. Although they still live across Canada and Alaska, they are not as widespread in the United States as they once were.

People are also the biggest threat to wild dogs and foxes. As well as direct persecution by farmers, many kinds of wild dogs and foxes have suffered from diseases such as anthrax that they have caught from domestic livestock. Another threat comes from trappers, who kill millions of foxes every year so that their pelts can be made into fashionable clothes.

CONFLICT WITH FARMERS

Ranchers and farmers keep livestock in numbers that would rarely be found in nature. This is a great temptation to a predator. Coyotes, jackals, and foxes, as well as wolves, are considered to be pests by farmers, although sometimes these bad reputations are not deserved. Some of the livestock eaten may have died from other causes. Also, wolves, wild dogs, and foxes help to reduce the numbers of other pests, such as rats, mice, and rabbits.

ATTACKS ON LIVESTOCK

People often say that wild dogs and foxes kill for the sake of killing when they get inside a poultry house. In the wild, a predator is able to chase and kill only one victim at a time. The others are free to escape. Inside a building, prey cannot escape. The predator is confused, and responds by killing as many as possible.

THE FUR TRADE

As many as 20 species of wild dogs and foxes are still hunted for their fur. This continues, despite the extreme distaste many people have for the fur trade. Some foxes are trapped from the wild, but in some parts of the world where it is still legal, fur farms breed species such as the Arctic fox. In some places in the United States, fur trapping results in the unintentional death of foxes.

NATURAL PREDATORS

The young pups of all species are vulnerable to predators, and so are all the smaller dogs and foxes. Such predators include birds of prey, snakes, lions, tigers, bears, and hyenas. In the United States, the gray fox is attacked and eaten by coyotes, mountain lions, and eagles. Kit foxes are caught by coyotes and red-tailed hawks.

A hen sitting on her nest is an easy catch for a stealthy red fox. People who keep hens have to make sure that they are well-protected.

Even a full-grown wolf may be in danger if it gets too close to a hungry grizzly bear, especially if it approaches a female with cubs.

HYBRIDS

A hybrid occurs when individual animals of two different species mate and produce offspring. Usually, different species are unable to breed, but because coyotes, wolves, dingoes, and domestic dogs are so closely related, they can interbreed successfully. Unfortunately, this affects the genetic purity of the wild species. The gray wolf population of Italy, although protected from persecution since 1977, is now threatened by inbreeding with domestic dogs.

DISEASE

Wild animals are affected by diseases in just the same way as domestic livestock. But diseases usually spread more slowly among animals in the wild. Domestic livestock and dogs are kept at much higher densities, so diseases can reach epidemic proportions and be transmitted to wild animals. Rabies, anthrax, and distemper threaten species such as African wild dogs and side-striped and other jackals.

CHAPTER 8
People and the Wolf Family

People have had a long and close association with the descendants of gray wolves—our domestic dogs. Most domestic dogs today are pets—friendly animals that enjoy human company. But domestication probably started when people realized that dogs made hunting easier. Besides dogs such as retrievers, pointers, and spaniels, which are still used by hunters, domestic dogs are now trained to fill a variety of other roles. Some are working dogs, used to guard property, round up sheep, or help the police. Huskies are still

A boy and his dog make good companions. Both are always ready to run around and play ball games.

The red wolf is the most endangered member of the dog family. It was declared extinct in 1980 but has since been reintroduced to the wild.

The last wild Falkland Islands wolf, or warrah, died in 1876.

The Siberian Husky is the breed of domestic dog closest in appearance to the gray wolf.

The tallest dog is the Irish wolfhound, which measures up to 40 inches (100 cm) at the shoulder. It was once used to hunt wolves.

Gray wolves were re-introduced into Yellowstone National Park in 1995.

Swift foxes, declared extinct in Canada in 1978, were re-introduced there, as part of an endangered species program, in 1983.

used in parts of the Arctic to pull sleds. Dogs can also be trained to help and guide people who have a variety of physical challenges.

Because they are such adaptable animals, able to live in many different kinds of places and eat many different kinds of food, few species are endangered or threatened with extinction. But some kinds do need help if they are to survive in the wild.

Sled dogs were once the only means of pulling heavy loads over Arctic ice. Nowadays, dogsledding is often a sport rather than a way of life.

Interbreeding with domestic dogs has proved to be a threat to the purity of species such as dingoes, and in some places, populations of gray wolves. Conservation schemes are underway to help endangered red wolves as well as other wild dogs and some rare foxes.

DOMESTIC DOGS

The domestication of the gray wolf began over 12,000 years ago. All domestic dogs are descended from the wolf. Across its wide natural range, the gray wolf is quite variable in appearance, from the large, pale timber wolves of North America to the smaller, browner wolf of eastern Europe and Asia. Today, there is a huge number of recognized breeds of domestic dog, although very many pets are mongrels—a mixture of breeds.

To a bulldog fancier, this female and her pup are perfect examples of the breed. Even so, breeding for specific physical characteristics often causes health problems in this breed and others.

The range in size, shape, and color of our pet dogs is considerable. There are long-haired dogs and short-haired dogs, in all colors and patterns. Some, such as miniature poodles, Scottish terriers, and the smallest dog of all, the Chihuahua, are so unlike their distant wolf ancestors that it is hard to imagine that they are still able to interbreed with each other! Unfortunately, over-breeding to produce "fashionable" dogs has led to health problems for some dogs. Bulldogs now have such flattened faces that they have breathing and chewing difficulties. Many breeds have hip problems or difficulties in giving birth.

CONSERVATION

The Convention on International Trade in Endangered Species (CITES) is an international treaty drawn up to control or prevent trade in endangered or vulnerable species of animals. The red wolf and the bush dog are completely protected. Trade in the pelts of eight other species of wild dogs, wolves, and foxes is strictly regulated by the treaty. This list includes the dhole; the maned wolf and several other kinds of foxes, including the fennec; and in some areas, the gray wolf.

Though it is protected by CITES, diseases caught from domestic dogs and persecution by farmers still threaten the maned wolf. Teaching farmers more about the natural diet of the maned wolf will help to calm their fears and reduce persecution.

CAPTIVE BREEDING

Endangered species that can be bred in zoos and wildlife parks can sometimes be released back into the wild. Provided that the habitat needed by these species is also protected, it is hoped that such captive-breeding programs can prevent extinction. Breeding programs for the red wolf, the African wild dog, and the bush dog are underway.

SPREADING NATURALLY

Populations of some wild dogs and foxes are spreading naturally. The raccoon dog once lived only in Siberia, China, and Japan but has

It is time for this captive-bred red wolf to be released back into the wild. Scientists often fit collars with radio tags, so they can track where the wolves go and how well they survive.

now spread into parts of Europe. The red fox successfully lives in cities in Europe and has also been seen occasionally in cities such as New York and Toronto. It is easy for red foxes to find food in cities. They feed on kitchen scraps and garbage, often raided from garbage cans. Red foxes seldom cause problems. Contrary to popular belief, they are unlikely to attack pet cats, although they would eat a cat killed by a car. In fact, young foxes and cats have often been seen playing together.

Return of the Wolf

Some conservationists think that the gray wolf ought to be reintroduced into parts of its range where it has become extinct, such as the western United States and Scotland. Would this be a good idea? There are many issues involved. Wolves need a large territory in order to survive, and they need to hunt for prey. In today's world, what was once wilderness is now ranchland, farms, or other human settlements. Farmers do not want wolves. They say that their livestock would be endangered, and that they would need compensation to cover their losses. Who should pay for this?

Glossary

ALPHA FEMALE – The female mate of the alpha male

ALPHA MALE – The dominant male in a dog pack

BINOCULAR VISION – Coordinated use of both eyes to judge size and distance accurately

CARNIVORE – Animal that eats the flesh of other animals

CARRION – Flesh of a dead animal, either one that has died naturally, or one that is the remains of another predator's kill

DEN – The shelter of a wolf, wild dog, or fox; a den may be in a tree, in a cave, or in the ground

DOMESTICATION – Adaptation of a wild animal to life in close contact with human beings

EXTINCT – When an animal species no longer exists; today, the phrase "extinct in the wild" is often used because individual animals of a species are sometimes kept alive in zoos after the animal has become extinct in nature

HYBRID – Offspring born to parent animals of two different species

INSULATION – A substance, such as fur or fat, that helps an animal keep heat in its body

LITTER – Offspring born to the same animal at the same time

MAMMALS – Animals with fur, whose young feed on milk produced by the mother

MOLT – To shed fur, feathers, or skin

MUZZLE – The projecting front part of an animal's face, made up of the mouth and nose

NOCTURNAL – Active at night

PACK – A group of wolves or wild dogs that live and hunt together

PELT – The skin of an animal

PREDATOR – An animal that catches and eats other animals

PREY – An animal that is caught and eaten by another animal

REGURGITATE – To vomit or expel food that has already been swallowed

RETINA – The layer at the back of the eyeball that is sensitive to light

SCENT-MARKING – Method used by an animal to mark its territory with its droppings or urine

SPECIES – A kind or type of animal

TAPETUM LUCIDUM – A layer behind the retina of many nocturnal mammals, including wolves, wild dogs, and foxes

TERRITORY – The area of land that an animal or pack occupies

VIXEN – A female fox

Further Reading

Dahl, Michael. *Wolf*. Danbury, CT: Children's Press, 1997.

George, Jean Craighead. *Look to the North:* A Wolf Pup Diary. New York: HarperCollins, 1998.

Ling, Mary. *Amazing Wolves, Dogs, and Foxes*. New York: Random House, 1995.

Perry, Phyllis. *Crafty Canines: Coyotes, Foxes, and Wolves*. Danbury, CT: Franklin Watts, 1999.

Zeaman, John. *How the Wolf Became a Dog*. New York: Franklin Watts, 1998.

Acknowledgments
Front cover: John Shaw/Bruce Coleman Collection; p.9: Staffan Widstrand/Bruce Coleman Collection; p.10: Press-tige Pictures/Oxford Scientific Films; p.11 Erwin & Peggy Bauer/Animals Animals/Oxford Scientific Films; p.12: HPH Photography/Bruce Coleman Collection; p.13: Kim Taylor/Bruce Coleman Collection; p.14: HPH Photography/Bruce Coleman Collection; p.16: Gunter Ziesler/Bruce Coleman Collection; p.17: Gerard Lacz/Natural History Photographic Agency; p.18: Richard & Julia Kemp/Survival Anglia/Oxford Scientific Films; p.19: Hans Reinhard/Bruce Coleman Collection; p.20: Peter Pickford/Natural History Photographic Agency; p.21: K.Ghani/ Natural History Photographic Agency; p.22: Christopher Ratier/Natural History Photographic Agency; p.23: Werner Layer/Bruce Coleman Collection; p.24: Rod Williams/Bruce Coleman Collection; p.25: Stephen J.Krasemann/Bruce Coleman Collection; p.26: Ben Osborne/Oxford Scientific Films; p.28: Jane Burton/Bruce Coleman Collection; p.29: Owen Newman/Oxford Scientific Films; p.30: Alan & Sandy Carey/Oxford Scientific Films; p.31: Daniel J.Cox/Oxford Scientific Films; p.32: Andy Rouse/Natural History Photographic Agency; p.33: Richard Day/Oxford Scientific Films; p.34: Darek Karp/Natural History Photographic Agency; p.35: Sophy & Michael Day/Bruce Coleman Collection; p.36: Daniel Heuclin/Natural History Photographic Agency; p.37: Daniel J.Cox/Oxford Scientific Films; p.38: Chris Fairclough; p.39: Staffan Widstrand/Bruce Coleman Collection; p.40: Adriano Bacchella/Bruce Coleman Collection; p.41: Erwin & Peggy Bauer/Bruce Coleman Collection; p.42: Stephan Krasemann/Natural History Photographic Agency; p.43: Hans Reinhard/Bruce Coleman Collection.

Index

Numbers in *italic* indicate pictures